LOVE &
SURGERY

To Don with fondness & admiration for your work. Thanks for coming to listen.

LOVE & SURGERY

VICTOR ENNS

Vancouver
Oct 3/2019

radiant press

Copyright @ 2019 Victor Enns

All rights reserved. No part of this publication may be reproduced, stored in a retrieval system or transmitted, in any form or by any means without the prior written permission of the publisher or by licensed agreement with Access: The Canadian Copyright Licensing Agency (contact accesscopyright.ca).

Editor: Sharon Thesen
Cover art: Murray Toews
Book and cover design: Tania Wolk, Third Wolf Studio
Printed and bound in Canada at Friesens, Altona, MB

The publisher gratefully acknowledges the support of Creative Saskatchewan.

Acknowledgements: Some of these poems have appeared in Prairie Fire, Jerry Jazz Musician and Shot Glass Journal (online, US). This collection was completed with the assistance of the Manitoba Art Council, family and friends.

Library and Archives Canada Cataloguing in Publication

Title: Love & surgery / Victor Enns.
Other titles: Love and surgery
Names: Enns, Victor, 1955- author.
Identifiers: Canadiana (print) 20190158379 | Canadiana (ebook) 20190158417 |
ISBN 9781989274118
(softcover) | ISBN 9781989274125 (PDF)
Subjects: LCGFT: Poetry.
Classification: LCC PS8559.N57 L68 2019 | DDC C811/.54—dc23

radiant press

Box 33128 Cathedral PO, Regina, SK S4T 7X2
info@radiantpress.ca   www.radiantpress.ca

to Lynn

To try to write love is to confront the muck of language: that region of hysteria where language is both too much and too little, excessive and impoverished.
– Roland Barthes

We heard Anne Carson read from her nearly new collection
The Beauty of The Husband, we bought, you paid.
Carson inscribed it to both of us, the beautiful wife, &
the third husband. The book went missing after you left.
What else can I make of that, you took it
leaving me with the songs of our wedding night & a picture of your kiss.

LOVE

Coffee Date ---- 6
Revelation ---- 7
The Green Mill ---- 8
Salsa Lessons ---- 9
Driving Home ---- 10
Hesitance ---- 11
When A Plan Comes Together ---- 12
Evidence ---- 13
A Good Fit ---- 14
Courage ---- 15
Love is coming ---- 16
Back in the Garden ---- 17
Love in this Morning ---- 18
Take Me Home ---- 19
Kites ---- 20
Landscaping ---- 21
You are Cold ---- 22
There is Never Enough ---- 23
After Hearing Leonard Cohen ---- 24
Left Behind with a Dog and a Limp ---- 25
Night Train ---- 26
Arrhythmia ---- 27
Miracle on Lenore Street ---- 28
Listen ---- 29
Music for Men Over Fifty ---- 30

SURGERY

Waiting for Dr. Hammond - 34
Dreaming Dr. Hammond - 35
Camera Shy - 37
Torpor - 39
Laughing Man - 40
My Left Foot - 41
Prosection - 42
Phantom Pain - 43
Malaise - 44
Elevated Conversation - 45
With My Eyes Closed - 46
Donor - 47
Keeping Time - 48
My Body Says - 51

COMPLICATIONS

The First Stone - 54
Reading Pablo Neruda - 55
Night Table - 56
Scar Tissue - 57
Reading Anne Carson - 58
Making My Bed - 60
Reading Mary Oliver - 61

LOVE

Exuberance is Beauty
– William Blake.

COFFEE DATE

You come get me, my son not back in time,
leaving me nothing but my fedora in hand.

Barzula espresso whines through the machines.
Your daughter happens by, gives me the once over

while you wait for your Australian flat white
in Bar Italia, still smelling of last night's beer.

I pass muster. Burn my tongue on my Americano.
We add what we need; nothing much, being human

we know the look of love. We hear Krall's voice distant
as Dusty, house speakers crackling memories of 1967.

REVELATION

The sunlight on the road to Chicago turns us
toward each other, stories full in our mouths.

There is room in the hatchback for what we need,
growing in the music of Al Green and Norah Jones.

Ahead of ourselves, we hold hands
while dusk settles her skirt around us.

In Chicago, the car empty of all but the moon,
we dream more jazz, less blues.

THE GREEN MILL

You are amused by my passion
for taxicabs. Their drivers always
know where we are going.

We don't need a map to get to this
whiskey bar. The Green Mill as old
as the jazz brought up river.

Notes bend around the two of us,
bring us love we left home to find;
we begin to improvise.

SALSA LESSONS

You take off your glasses
to read novels – or me, in bed.

We put out the light: the room full
of close air, Cuban salsa loud, and hot,

so the kids won't hear us searching
for rhythm in the winter night.

DRIVING HOME

Bucking snowdrifts I think
of rising to meet you two nights ago.

In the dark your want found
my need; all the light

inside where we met
the night. Nerve steady

I turn my head, both hands
on the wheel, yours casting off.

HESITANCE

There is a risk
nothing will come
of this, my reach
limited.

Dislocated,
my shoulder remembers
light armour, my arm
amour.

WHEN A PLAN COMES TOGETHER

You sketch your plans
on graph paper,
I rearrange the alphabet.

Our conclusions are
the same love.
Our perspectives

draw us closer
from two different
hemispheres.

We make our way
out of our heads
into each other.

EVIDENCE

Undone, my New Balance size 14 cross-trainers
come off. I relax and remove my leather braces,
whip off my socks, and expose my collapsing feet.

Riddled with screws and scars they give evidence
I cannot stand alone. Tenderly you reach for me.
My body seeks sensation, alive under your hands.

A GOOD FIT

Prescribed drugs bring me
into you as alive
as a slippery fish
arcing
out of water
pleasure in the leap
one element
to another

COURAGE

It has started to snow. The road through the park is icy.
A fox, caught in my headlights, drifts into the forest

taking my fear into the dark. I once was a lover
the snow a brilliant idea for angels to sleep on.

Once a lover, you cross a thousand mile ocean, sun at your back.
Winter takes your breath away. You choose a Husky at the pound.

You wash our sheets, our beautiful scars.
we are lovers, once, again.

LOVE IS COMING

Man over fifty is less
sure than twenty, when he knew
everything, and didn't need
reassurance about the beauty
of his tic tock measuring time.

The inadequacy of the flesh
in the face of love, hold over
of Adam's surprise; and me still
telling lies. Scrabbling for Viagra
O God of Pharma, realize me.

BACK IN THE GARDEN

Love hands me a spade, knowledge
gained from the bent back rather
than snakes. Still, a woman stands
beside me under a crabapple tree.

She has her hopes up, this Australian transplant
for her first Canadian garden with a man
who hates to get his hands dirty, but promises
to go where she goes, even if it's

a Wolseley backyard full of weeds
from a decade of neglect. Right now
it's time for new stories and perennials,
the live fuse the live flower driving love.

LOVE IN THIS MORNING

There is love in this morning
between us, moving to daylight
though bed and children protest.

We slip together, hand in glove,
waking to touch, we've got each other's
back, letting go.

We leave our old countries,
you're a long way back. I wait
for my passport, birth certificate

changed again. This time
renewed, my luxurious heart
makes room, makes room
for you.

TAKE ME HOME

When I am nowhere
dissociating
in this crowded
farmers' market
next to you
is the safest place
to be me,
relocated again.

KITES

A strong west wind takes our kites
up into blue sky just ahead of us.

Ollie cuts the lawn. It's been mostly dry
& windy these last three days. The sun is bright –

your kite makes straight for it, pulling
the reel out of your hands and into power

lines marking off the prairie still visible
here, away from the lake rustling like crinoline –

my kite crashes on the lawn. Yours captured
by Manitoba Hydro. We settle in,

words like "the long haul" are off limits, though
there is no capriciousness in our love

as we bet on how long
the box kite will stay in the air.

LANDSCAPING

I see you in the garden, digging in the heat.
Your children set the gateposts, fencing the backyard.

My camera realizes distance between us. I see you
& your children through a lens and our repaired windows.

Turning my head I see a homeless man step down
the street holding his hands before him as if they held

the Holy Grail. Later this evening, close
and humid, you are what I have to hold.

YOU ARE COLD

to me this morning. You turn your back. You have broad shoulders,
so you've told me, but this morning enough is enough. You say
my drinking stretches on, & like this long winter it's too much.

Your disappointment raises a risk I keep taking, with love,
and with lovers. "If only," I've heard, "he could keep away
from the hard stuff." You leave the bed early, have a hot shower.

You turn to the wall of closets, choosing something warm
for Winnipeg's endless winter, leaving your perfume in the air.

THERE IS NEVER ENOUGH

Love, this fragrant afternoon
is hidden in hibiscus, found
as I look for you in the flowers
you brought from the nursery
down the street. The dog has escaped
again, throwing herself
in front of a family sedan,
the anxious driver on her cell
in a hurry to get her kids to practice.
I refuse to chase
the representations of love –
put away my notebook & sunglasses.
Your honest body is what I crave,
racing pulse when I see you
move, show a little skin
in your sleeveless floral top.
You platter the poached wild salmon
unwrap the foil, as we listen to love songs
carried uncertainly by the afternoon breeze.
We lift our cold white Marlborough wine,
our glasses cheer the day.

AFTER HEARING LEONARD COHEN

A fine evening, this night the snow lightly falling,
as my hand finds the edge of your skirt.

It's Friday night and Portage Avenue.
We're on our way home, the house empty.

Our children are out in the night
following their instincts, dreams left

for later. Inside we become naked, lie
against each other warming the space

between us. We move the dark
to the outside of love.

LEFT BEHIND WITH A DOG AND A LIMP

You've gone to Toronto, taking your son,
leaving his dog, a family reminder
straining against the leash.

This city not big or wise enough holds me,
while the dog pulls me through the days
I'm waiting to be over. My memory

impaired, my walking too, as I wobble
my way around the block shuffling
through the fallen leaves.

NIGHT TRAIN[1]

The house is full
and us in it. We
make room
for each
other.

No illusions
we know
time is
to touch
each other.

We hear the jazz
taking on the night
train, rocking
the moon.

1 *Night Train,* Oscar Peterson, released 1963

ARRHYTHMIA

You have taken the rubber mallet
to the cracked wall plaster,
dusting the hardwood under your knees.

I'm looking to name your epithalamium
 & all I can hear is the banging
of your hammer, angry with me.

I am not a carpenter, not handy with much
but the turn of a phrase, you don't want my
fine excuses, in writing

or in law. Too late for apology, I offer
my irregular heart. Just a little jazz later
tonight, *Moonglow* plays

quietly, with soft touch, my hope & my wish
for you to love me without good reason;
My Crazy Love Your Blues in the Night.

MIRACLE ON LENORE STREET

The first morning
of this New Year
I wake to wake
you into this
little miracle
shudder, provenance
as hazy as the smoke
of last night's
cigar.

LISTEN

I have nothing new to say, but know
we both listen to these songs,
ancient and bold,

we have all we need music,
to make love our own
shucking oysters

to the music of longing,
centuries old.

like the ocean.
Between us

at the sink.

MUSIC FOR MEN OVER FIFTY
for Etta James

1.
I look for my pajamas, slip them over
my swollen ankles, over my rash salved
with steroid cream, my skin starting to thin,
starting to sag and fold like crepe streamers.
Lame, I am deaf to being *enabled*, hammering
to pieces my Phonak hearing aids with my right brace.

2.
This morning, I wake to music from the Acoustic Research clock radio.
Music I've loved since I was old enough to love the way a woman moves
in front of the mirror when she thinks I'm not looking. I'm always looking,
disconcerting my wife who feels the same way about her belly as I do
about mine, but in a more feminine way, or so I'd like to think.
We smile at each other in the glass, side by side, love a hardship
we endure.

3.
How to praise your children who leave us alone to love
on this Saturday night, the Acoustic Research radio playing
the songs accompanying us to Chicago. Remember me happy
in a cab, jazz at the Green Mill, the Beetle back in the hotel parking lot.

Roll with me honey, in your dreams
roll me, honey, in your dreams.

True, it's been awhile, and longer than I would want
but there are so many excuses, so many reasons
I choose to sleep. Not enough blood in the old
pecker so many nights. You prefer love in the dark

Roll with me honey, in your dreams
roll me, honey, in your dreams.

4.

I am early to rise in the morning, just not convincing in the light. We hold on to what we love, often enough each other, when we can see past our own mistakes, finding what it was that took us down the I-94.

Roll with me honey, in your dreams
roll me, honey, in your dreams.

SURGERY

A wound gives off its own light surgeons say.
– Anne Carson, *The Beauty of the Husband*

WAITING FOR DR. HAMMOND

Mr. Ballantine[2]; my shrink says I should write about you,
but that is a lie. He thinks I should write about the betrayal
of my body as it begins to break down ahead of schedule.

Every morning now I struggle into my braces described by my physio
as if they were guy wires holding up a tree not quite capable of standing
up by itself. Why, George, do I not find this reassuring though there are days

I feel as big as a tree, but filled with ants and rot, just plain tired
of being a tree. The leaves I turn are in a book called Freedom.
I call the one doctor in town who may be able to replace my ankle

with a titanium joint and reach only an answering machine, Wait
is the answer, six to nine months. Wait – a lesson my father
tried to leave with me in his dying.

---

2 George (A. Ballantine = Ballantine's whisky.)

DREAMING DR. HAMMOND

1. I'm unlaced, enjoying a chair in the corner,
my feet a small disaster of perspective
which I do not hold.

I shake powders, apply salves,
ointments, call for the curator
of the crippled, claim I have nothing

for which I should apologize:
just the desire to keep walking,
climb the stairs to my bed.

2. Yes, says the Doctor of Bones
*fusion will do for a stumper
as young and fat as you.*

He sends his resident to explain
there is a thirty percent failure rate
for complete recovery,

a ten percent rate of do-overs,
fixing what didn't work the first time,
and one percent failure, three out of 300.

3. Dreaming my body hosts surgeons
like a black and white 1960s cocktail party,

surgeons all men, three olives
in their martinis. I dream their wives

& their nurses with cinched waists
& clenched fists, grasping

Bloody Marys, bend
just one more night,

to the godliness of the knife
in the surgeon's hand –

uncover my body –
their banquet on the table.

CAMERA SHY

To photograph is to confer importance.
– Susan Sontag

1.
My angry fascination with the abyss,
with the edge, cutting or leading,
comes to this; I sit on the ledge
of the soaker tub, swing my legs
into the hot blue water, my back
hunched, my hands on the grab bars
lowering a body mass index close to obese.

Risk management, a skill listed
on my resume to keep on living,
insists on the rubber mat, stones
just a picture under my ass
as if my rejuvenation would not be
complete without misrepresentation.

2.
The photographer knocks, and I say
come in. My face does not know
what to do in front of a camera;
my body long past
caring; only the surgeons,
planning their cuts, need to know.

3.
The photographer breaks up
with me, an inadequate subject
my face empty of expression
or nuance, nothing going on
the lens can see, no conflict –
all cameras attracted to danger,
nothing doing here, my vacancy
a flat effect, only I feel the black dog
paratroopers drop behind my eyes.

TORPOR

Hours of near unconsciousness, a knockdown so heavy
I cannot get up on my knees to pray or weed my brain
irrigated by the pharmaceuticals I crack
out of my blister pack & slap into my mouth by the handful.
I can hardly keep my eyes open, no hallucinations,
no delusions I am anyone other than I am, grinding
bones, breath and pain the only things
moving. The bullish orderlies lift me
still and slack in the Hoyer, swaying, suspended,
nowhere to take me or put me down. The bleached sheets
underneath my carcass, the nurse's hands
noncommittal as they lay me down, warts and all. Jesus, where are you?
I'm giving you the best Lazarus I've got.
Let me stand up and walk.

LAUGHING MAN

She read me like my own book,
the one I gave to her. Days later,
she said she read it through
and through.

She said *I see a lifetime
of suffering after*, yes that's
what she said, a lifetime
of suffering.

But no one would know.
You don't show it, she said
you laugh so much. I said
what's a lifetime of suffering –
without a sense of humour
there can be no sense at all.

MY LEFT FOOT

Make no bones about it; my left foot carried its final edition
in my genes since the day I was born. My left ankle's collapse
a birth defect; its ankle fusion fix a failure, confirmed too late
by a CT scan for anyone to believe my foot's pain was 9 on a scale
of 1 to 10. There is bigger and better suffering everywhere,
this close to the end times, pictures of fire and famine eclipse
the sagging memory of my ragged metatarsal,
bone giving way, under the operating theatre lights.

PROSECTION

I remain unconcerned about whether I signed away my foot
to teach medical students a lesson. I'm more worried
about losing sleep. I can hear the party that night,
me not invited to dance. These young students, humans so alive
their skin is skin-tight even when they move. Mine continues
its crepe-y sag on the calf of the right leg I have remaining
below the knee. Was it just yesterday I could feel the surgeon
pulling on my left foot, I said, "hey, you're pulling my leg."
I had very good drugs. Still, I didn't hear anybody laughing.

I could laugh about it then, and still do with the same detached concern
dissociation brings when part of you is missing. Whatever phantoms
of the body opera are lurking have yet to expose themselves. As I balance
on my new prosthesis, this morning the students remember my ankle in pieces.

PHANTOM PAIN

My shrink was thinking he was telling me something I didn't know.
If they amputate your left foot, you may still be left
with the pain. Ah phantom pain, I say. I heard about that on television.

I'll have to treat it with phantom pharmaceuticals while mindfully
looking at my stump, mindfully receiving the information that I have no
left foot, any phantom pain likely from my surgeon's prosection

each failed screw a learning opportunity as they come away
from the bone. Yes I can imagine that phantom pain just enough below
to kneel on. I read our separation agreement, noting the absence of you

mindfully noting the absence of my foot reconciling the thought of pain
as I see nothing leaving something, a phantom, like I wrote once in 1985,
now more consciously aware of the phantom pain left by your leaving

for Australia. My pain stays here; my work calls me to stay here.
Too many mistakes getting this far for my betrayal to be pardoned.
I get it, while the dishwater circles the sink, grey-water draining into sand.

MALAISE

Pain early morning onset oxycodone won't spell itself
rack racked back cracking my lame brain used to be
an epithet finding its way to lame ass lame is miserable
lame is chronic lame is laconic lame is iconic pirating
in the stifling heat and haze, now elbow now knee
got to do got to get up got to jump into the fire[3]

3 Harry Nilsson

ELEVATED CONVERSATION

Two children on foot scooters glance sideways, see
I am short a foot. "What happened?" asks blue jacket.
"There was a problem with my foot, they tried to fix it,
but couldn't, so they cut it off."
"Did they use a chainsaw?"
"No" red sweater says, "no. I bet they used a power saw though!"
"Sorta kinda" I said, "and now they are making me a new leg."
"You should get them to make you a pirate leg!" says blue jacket.
"AARRGH!" they shout together as the elevator lets them out.

WITH MY EYES CLOSED

1.
Protecting my soul, I close my eyes in the face of new pain centers.
Every time I get up, God pulls out another Jenga block,
while head nuns steady me wobbling to my feet.
It's true you cross the street, rather than be seen walking with this cripple.
Honesty is important, you said, but you lied anyway, to save my feelings.
In my feet ? Honestly dearie, I have none. But thanks for the gelato.

2.
My eyes close to black; spiked by flashes of neuropathic pain they warn you about
if you have amputation. I have the pain already, maybe the surgeon
could make it disappear like my left foot. All I want is a prosthetic.
"I can walk!" I want to shout, lying to the revivalist in a tent crusade,
throwing away my crutch. But for now, the circus, the freak show and
the strongman slamming the sledgehammer on the lever of the high-striker,
the steel puck rippling up every vertebra, before ringing the bell in my brain.

DONOR

Just as soon as I cinch up my brace
pain comes barreling down the pipe
to the new end of my leg, blurts out
unruly messages slipping and slapping
whipping and snapping with a heavy pulley
winched in my heart I don't let go heavy
I don't let go easy; I don't let anyone know
I gather this flailing energy into new parts
of my three quarters self, donating my body
to science one limb at a time.

KEEPING TIME

Soon, I discover pain
sets its hours, a daily routine
modulated by the pills the doctors hate
to give me, convinced from the first
I am an addict, or worse –
their script will make me one.

I learn to wear the lie confidently
on my face, one or two tablets
every six hours for 20 days, that's all
Though you and your doctor know one
is not enough for the size of pain
on a 236 pound frame. So I count

the hours, holding on to the relief
of the bath in the morning, taking
the first two tablets at 8:00 a.m.,
though not always, just never later. By 9:00 a.m.
I breathe normally, unclenching

safely at my desk, working for a good
two hours, the computer digits ticking
over in my brain like a Bergman clock,
striking 11:00. Wordless, pain throws his jacket
in my reading chair where I can no longer
read at any hour, taking just a minute

to sharpen his fingernails. Pain sizes me up
like every bullyboy I ever knew
giving his best hour to my skin and bones.
The clock strikes noon, the NSAIDS with food,
the two oxycodone tablets, filtered water
poured over just the right amount of ice.

Flat on my back I listen to Radio 2,
moving Fiona, my heating pad,
to the joints where pain
prefers to hang out, forcing him to leave,
with his Terminator smile,
knowing he will be back at 4:00.

The 4 o' clock variations: you're so far away

I shut down my computer, turn down
the music I have heard too often,
songs I want to hear again for the first
time, turning the clock back, but
now you are so far away from me
just a chorus in an old pop song.

It's late so I practice my dialogues
complete with hand gestures, so many
need convincing. Pain jeers at my failures,
slips the knife in my hand, unlike my father
chopping vegetables mindlessly,
waiting for the blood to run.

MY BODY SAYS

My body says scream, my body says pain, my body says
groan, my body says grunt – grunt louder than Rafael Nadal!
My body says take that, my body says heavy, my body says
stumble, my body says slip, my body says fall, my ankle says fracture.

My surgeon says surgery, says plate, says screws, my body says pain, my body says
grunt – grunt louder than Rafael Nadal! My body says you idiot, my body says
limp, my body says I give, says give me opioids, my surgeon says get a prescription
from someone else. My body says "What, get a prescription from someone else?"

My body says osteoid-arthritis, my body says I'll grind your bones until you're dead,
my body says you will fulfill your father's prophecy, buried in your
genes, my body says shout, my body says scream, my body says
groan, my body says grunt – grunt louder than Rafael Nadal!

My foot surgeon says stage four flatfoot, my surgeon says foot fusion, my surgeon says
feet first, my surgeon says hips later, my surgeon says wait, my surgeon says left right, says
pins in your hammertoes, my body says "What? Pins in my hammertoes?!" My body says
groan, my body says grunt – grunt louder than Rafael Nadal!

My body says polyneuropathy, my body says my body electric, my body says flail like
downed hydro lines during a Montreal ice storm, my body says pain, my body says
scream, my body says shout, my body says groan, my body says
grunt – grunt louder than Rafael Nadal!

My surgeon says ankle fusion, my surgeon says you're screwed, my surgeon says slow recovery, my surgeon says your left ankle has failed, my surgeon says replacement, my surgeon says tricky, I say, just cut it off. Surgeon says, "What? Cut if off?" My body says groan my body says
grunt – grunt louder than Rafael Nadal!

My body says pain, my body says scream, my body says
shout, my body says groan, my body says
grunt – grunt louder than Rafael Nadal!

My body says scream, my body says groan, my body says
grunt – grunt louder than Rafael Nadal!
Louder than Rafael Nadal!

COMPLICATIONS

Pain is always new to those who suffer,
but loses its originality for those around them.
– Alphonse Daudet[4]

La doulou: (la douleur), 1887-1895 (Paris: Librairie de France, 1930) p. 16; Julian Barnes (ed. and trans.) In the Land of Pain (New York: Alfred A. Knopf, 2002) p. 19

THE FIRST STONE

…You will be touching what I have touched…
Roland Barthes

You took my hand in the planetarium theatre, drawing connections in my palm
the first time we watched a film about climate change and the end of the world.

Me like always, in a hurry, no time to lose, my euphoria generating more thoughts
than the next morning could hold, one kept coming back over and over again

like a bad cliché, buy a ring, and propose.

My psychiatrist was right. Too early he said, there are more romantic places
than Ducky's Fish and Chips. So I waited until we reached the Exchange.

For dessert, we had cake, and ate it too. Over black coffee, my Viennese,
you with a flat white, I proffered my gift — my hand for yours.

No you said. Taking the ring, and slipping it on the other hand.
Not now you said. I thought, a good fit. I can wait, I lied to myself.

READING PABLO NERUDA

2007
Across from me near the birch wood fire
you read Pablo Neruda, nurse your bandaged
ring finger cut opening the bacon for breakfast.

Bach is fugue-ing and I look at you in front of the window
full of September and Lake Winnipeg
wonder how long can this be true.

2014
Listening to the fugue, again, this morning as the oxycodone lifts
pain from my bones, I want new memories as good as the old
for you and for me. Where changing position, deepens me

in you, and is not another way for my bones to lie. I don't want the rest,
I want you, this morning, the sun rising over the water; inside
the kettle whistling, a cup of tea what I have to offer.

NIGHT TABLE

Around midnight the wrong wife visits naked. Wrong wrong in his head
his proper current and lively wife asleep beside him, but neither he
or she wakes to accuse the spirit of his philandering. Australia new
to him no ghosts, he expected no ghosts dreaming in this new continent.
Too much red wine and red meat perfectly cooked and presented,
much too late after a day on the Great Ocean Road, nearby
restaurant recommended by the desk clerk of our roadside motel.

Checking out I thanked the clerk for his recommendation,
persuading my beautiful wife to have a breakfast there as well.
We've just got our coffees, placed our order when the motel manager
comes up to us and asks, "These yours?" spilling out her jewelry
including engagement and wedding rings onto the table. Forgotten
in the night table. Her spirit too, may have gone a wandering. Before
we learn the manager's name he has slipped away booking another dream.

SCAR TISSUE

You order a flat white at Bar I, meeting me to sign the separation agreement, with a
Scandinavian steel ring as big as a small satellite dish on your scarred fourth finger.

You found it in two pieces when you weren't looking for it. Your first ring,
an extravagance while you were still in design school, like the first husband.

The scar as well, the ring catching on a stair railing when you stumbled, a bad break,
bones pinned to hold your finger together, like my left hip when I was fourteen.

My hips replaced four decades later, this ring you begin to turn, stopped
by its size, replacing my grey pearl for your hand. The pearl in the ring is so worn

down it rolls in its metal, and will need to be replaced (like me, I think pathetically),
you tell me, but of your spoiled diamond ring, nothing to say. A wedding ring you chose,

you paid for, and will keep. I proffer my 18 karat-gold wedding ring
for an old debt. We murmur agreed, and look to our signatures.

READING ANNE CARSON

The blade of the Bergdorf knife is surprisingly sharp for something bought
at the thrift shop. BergHOFF Schinken Messer, my own translation
'for cutting pork from the bone.' 'Nothing fancy,' my mother would say,
brought over from the old country post-war, designed and made in Germany.

Standing rib roast on the carving board, beautiful meat, perfectly cooked
I could not wait to bite into the pink and bloody meat, and so hurried
to muscle the knife to cut a thin slice. My Yorkshire puddings achingly beautiful,
waiting, on the sideboard, for my disappointing gravy.

The knife blade slipped, though I had a mighty firm grip
on the handle, arthritis or no, the cut just above the knuckle
on my left ring finger. Stepped away from the meat, not wanting
to taste my own blood when I would eat. Our dog on the other hand

sniffed, and after slight hesitation licking up the considerable drippings
from my finger, following me through the house to the bathroom,
the medicine cabinet filled with boxes of bandages, elastic and fabric,
sterile non-stick, butterfly. We have them all.

You cut your finger in a kitchen on this very stretch of lakefront, ten years gone.
It was bacon we were after. Not a single bandage was found, so here now
a multitude of bandages and disinfectants. Difference,
I am alone, unable to stop the bleeding or bandage myself.
I wrap my injury tight with reams of Bounty, and drive the causeway
to Emergency where two indigenous nurses clean and bandage me properly,
no-one credentialed to stitch this weekend. That's alright I tell them,

a scar is just what the doctor ordered. Precisely when you are away, possibly
for good, my bad. This reminder, not to come off; like the gold wedding band
from Tiffany's, back in its box, in the night table coming to rest, bloodless
company for my second wedding band. I don't remember either being there.

MAKING MY BED

Back on the rack again waiting for sleep on the new sheets
you said were the same colour as those you first put on
our bed together ten years ago. I remember differently
choosing rust coloured bedding, which looked
even better with your auburn hair on the pillow.
I wrote courage I wrote scars, I wrote free to love again, &
now back where we started; you make my bed for the last time.

READING MARY OLIVER[5]

1.
You do not have to be good...

I'm having trouble not getting to my knees like we discussed
at our wedding. I don't have to be good but I should be
better than this. One hundred miles on my knees now
is easier than walking erect (ha), my feet my Achilles heel (ho).
Hot-blooded you prefer the desert; I was raised for repentance,
my cold blood slowly slugging through my irregular heart.

2.
You only have to let the soft animal of your body love what it loves.

There are fox here on Willow Island, likely two, hunting.
I am here too, hunting for an explanation that won't make your lip curl,
what animal eats what another has killed? "Crow," I hear Dyck saying,
fishing for cutthroats. I always thought I would be a prettier bird.

Mary, I think I'll go with Bukowski on this now that I am done with citizenry, fatherhood. Bukowski, Facebook tells me said, "Find out what you love and do it until it kills you." Tonight I set fire to all the rationalizations as to why I stopped writing poems to you, my beautiful wife. I reach again for the pear, the fallen crabapple, one fine line for another.

5 Italics, glossas source, quotations from the poem "Wild Geese" by Mary Oliver.

3.
Tell me about despair, yours, and I will tell you mine.

I should have replaced my hearing aids; even the ear
trumpet in the museum would let me hear your fear
of travelling alone, or losing sight on your return.
I took my pain to bed, not to Australia. I chose dark
but familiar company, my own self, here where willows bend.

In the pit, black dogs for company, vampire bats to eat,
I thought there was no further to fall. I was wrong,
the bottom fell out of the pit. I didn't
notice until there was enough momentum
to take my left foot below the knee, and
now I realize its pits all the way down.

4.
Meanwhile the sun and the clear pebbles of the rain
are moving across the landscapes...

This sweaty western afternoon sun is glorious, the Tanqueray
from the Duty Free, vermouth from the drugstore outside the park.
My improvised martini, stirred not shaken, a proper drink,
as I read your divorce petition. My glass sweats on the deck
of my brother's ranch style, ready for another pour. Tomorrow
I'll tell you the story about the vegan and the carnivore.

5.
Meanwhile the wild geese, high in the clean blue air,
are heading home again.

My last winter. I'm not waiting anymore. You are not coming back.

The pelicans are gone. The wild geese are gone, the two wild eagles that stayed
last winter have gone. The gophers have gone to ground even the mice have disappeared.
No sign of the red fox, and when it's this cold, there are no dogs outside.

Outside I fall heavily, on my right hip, but the artificial joint holds, my good news
for the day. I was trying to capture the heavy storm coming from the north
across Lake Winnipeg driving waves as sheets of ice over the cold grey stones.

Nothing broken, I roll on to my hands and knees, no-one to see me retrieve my shoe,
then the iPad. Nothing broken, I stumble again and again staying upright, until I reach
a chair in the summer porch to catch me. Breathing like there is no tomorrow.

Nobody is waiting. I sound as lame as I am made by my feet, my nerves
crackling with misdirected electrics, while my surgeon waits
for the CT scan of my unmoored and collapsing ankle.

6.
Whoever you are, no matter how lonely,
the world offers itself to your imagination...

The wild Canada geese fly south, taking the initial of my first name,
mocking my incomplete passport application, my inability to fly.
Yesterday nothing but dullness between us, my energy depleted at the speed
of dark, your exuberance overpowered by my sheer inertia. You finish packing
the last remains, your first initial in the suitcase sighing as it closes.
With a snap of its latches, you leave me the V and ampersand, your dog and Jo's cat.
Today I pass the preying bald eagle on a chunk of lake ice, the last snowbird to leave
this winter, so much colder than last. At the end of the road, my newspaper is gone,
the geese gone, the pelicans gone, the cottagers gone, you gone south.
Today I hold my face to the north wind, while the wipers play frozen
tag on the windshield. The heavy spume crosses the causeway making ice
on the fly. I repeat "Break, break, break against these cold grey rocks
oh Lake Winnipeg," turning in to what is still our driveway,
though there's only me to say "I'm home."

PHOTO CREDIT: MURRAY TOEWS

VICTOR ENNS graduated from the University of Manitoba in 1979 with a History/English major, including the advanced creative writing workshop with Robert Kroetsch, which led to the publication of his first poetry collection, *Jimmy Bang Poems* (Turnstone 1979). A founding Board member of the Manitoba Writers' Guild, he was the Executive Director of the Saskatchewan Writers' Guild from 1982 – 1988 and founder of *Windscript* magazine featuring the literary and visual art of Saskatchewan high school students. He spent the next 20 years in arts administration while also raising a family, taking time out to found *Rhubarb* magazine, a literary and visual arts magazine for writers and artists of Mennonite descent in 1998, returning as executive editor in 2012. His collection, *Afghanistan Confessions*, poems in the voices of Canadian soldiers, was released in November 2014. *boy*, was published in 2012. *Lucky Man*, was nominated in 2005 for the McNally Robinson Manitoba Book of the Year Award. Victor lives in Gimli, Manitoba.